Collins English Readers

Amazing Scientists

Level 4
CEF B2

Text by

D1394142

Collins

HarperCollins Publishers
77–85 Fulham Palace Road
Hammersmith London W6 8JB

10 9 8 7 6 5 4 3 2 1

Original text
© The Amazing People Club Ltd

Adapted text
© HarperCollins Publishers Ltd 2014

ISBN: 978-0-00-754500-1

Collins® is a registered trademark of
HarperCollins Publishers Limited

www.collinselt.com

A catalogue record for this book is available
from the British Library

Printed in the UK by Martins the Printers

All rights reserved. No part of this book
may be reproduced, stored in a retrieval
system, or transmitted in any form or
by any means, electronic, mechanical,
photocopying, recording or otherwise,
without the prior permission in writing
of the Publisher. This book is sold subject
to the conditions that it shall not, by way
of trade or otherwise, be lent, re-sold,
hired out or otherwise circulated without
the Publisher's prior consent in any form
of binding or cover other than that in
which it is published and without a similar
condition including this condition being
imposed on the subsequent purchaser.

HarperCollins does not warrant that
www.collinselt.com or any other website
mentioned in this title will be provided
uninterrupted, that any website will be
error free, that defects will be corrected, or
that the website or the server that makes it
available are free of viruses or bugs. For full
terms and conditions please refer to the site
terms provided on the website.

These readers are based on original texts
(BioViews®) published by The Amazing
People Club group.® BioViews® and The
Amazing People Club® are registered
trademarks and represent the views of the
author.

BioViews® are scripted virtual interview
based on research about a person's life and
times. As in any story, the words are only
an interpretation of what the individuals
mentioned in the BioViews® could have
said. Although the interpretations are
based on available research, they do not
purport to represent the actual views of
the people mentioned. The interpretations
are made in good faith, recognizing that
other interpretations could also be made.
The author and publisher disclaim any
responsibility from any action that readers
take regarding the BioViews® for educational
or other purposes. Any use of the BioViews®
materials is the sole responsibility of the
reader and should be supported by their own
independent research.

Cover image © Sergey Melnikov/
Shutterstock

MIX
**Paper from
responsible sources**

FSC **FSC™ C007454**
www.fsc.org

FSC™ is a non-profit international organisation established to promote the
responsible management of the world's forests. Products carrying the FSC
label are independently certified to assure consumers that they come from
forests that are managed to meet the social, economic and ecological needs
of present and future generations, and other controlled sources.

Find out more about HarperCollins and the environment at
www.harpercollins.co.uk/green

◆ CONTENTS ◆

Collins Amazing People Readers are collections of short stories. Each book presents the life story of five or six people whose lives and achievements have made a difference to our world today. The stories are carefully graded to ensure that you, the reader, will both enjoy and benefit from your reading experience.

You can choose to enjoy the book from start to finish or to dip in to your favourite story straight away. Each story is entirely independent.

After every story a short timeline brings together the most important events in each person's life into one short report. The timeline is a useful tool for revision purposes.

Words which are above the required reading level are underlined the first time they appear in each story. All underlined words are defined in the glossary at the back of the book. Levels 1 and 2 take their definitions from the *Collins COBUILD Essential English Dictionary* and levels 3 and 4 from the *Collins COBUILD Advanced English Dictionary*.

To support both teachers and learners, additional materials are available online at www.collinselt.com/readers.

The Amazing People Club®

Collins Amazing People Readers are adaptations of original texts published by The Amazing People Club. The Amazing People Club is an educational publishing house. It was founded in 2006 by educational psychologist and management leader Dr Charles Margerison and publishes books, eBooks, audio books, iBooks and video content which bring readers 'face to face' with many of the world's most inspiring and influential characters from the fields of art, science, music, politics, medicine and business.

◆ THE GRADING SCHEME ◆

The Collins COBUILD Grading Scheme has been created using the most up-to-date language usage information available today. Each level is guided by a brand new comprehensive grammar and vocabulary framework, ensuring that the series will perfectly match readers' abilities.

		CEF band	Pages	Word count	Headwords
Level 1	elementary	A2	64	5,000–8,000	approx. 700
Level 2	pre-intermediate	A2–B1	80	8,000–11,000	approx. 900
Level 3	intermediate	B1	96	11,000–15,000	approx. 1,100
Level 4	upper intermediate	B2	112	15,000–18,000	approx. 1,700

For more information on the Collins COBUILD Grading Scheme, including a full list of the grammar structures found at each level, go to www.collinselt.com/readers/gradingscheme.

Also available online: Make sure that you are reading at the right level by checking your level on our website (www.collinselt.com/readers/levelcheck).

Alessandro Volta

◆ ◆ ◆

1745–1827

the man who invented the battery

**Before electricity, people lived half their lives in darkness.
We relied on horses for transport. The basic ingredients
had been available for over 2,000 years, so why
did it take us so long to learn to use the power
of electricity?**

◆ ◆ ◆

On 18th February 1745, I was born into a wealthy family, in Como in northern Italy. Both my parents, my mother, Donna Maddalena and my father, Filippo, came from high-class Catholic families. I was a very <u>introverted</u> child, and even by the age of four, I wasn't speaking. My family thought that I was unable to speak, that I lacked the intelligence to do so. Despite this, I was sent to the local Catholic school, run by priests, and by the time I was seven, I had surprised everybody. Far from being stupid, I was really quite clever. At this time, my father died, which affected me deeply and

I became even quieter and less communicative. My uncle, who took over the responsibility for my education, and the teachers at school, wanted me to become a priest. This had been the career of other members of my family and it seemed suitable for me, too. I, however, was not interested in joining the church and I refused. My family's second career choice for me was law. I wasn't very keen on becoming a lawyer either. When I was fifteen, I started studying <u>natural philosophy</u> at school. I was a good student and I also liked reading and studying languages, something I appeared to be talented in because I learnt to speak Latin, French, English, Dutch, Spanish, Russian and Greek. I liked writing poetry, too. My real interests, however, were physics and chemistry.

I was fascinated by the way things worked and I read all the science books I could find, especially if they were about electricity, which I was really interested in. In 1763, when I was 18, I started to write letters to a French <u>physicist,</u> who was also a priest, called Jean-Antoine Nollet. Nollet had been doing experiments with electricity. In 1748, he had invented the electroscope – a machine that could find whether there was an electric charge present in something or not. He was also fond of demonstrating the results of his research and his lectures soon became popular. One spectacular demonstration was done in front of King Louis XV at the Palace of Versailles in France. Nollet managed to pass an electrical charge through 180 people. For this demonstration he used 180 soldiers and something called a Leyden jar. This was an ordinary glass jar which was lined with paper-thin sheets of tin – a metal, and three-quarters filled with water. At the top of the jar there was a cork through which passed a thin metal wire. The wire was attached to a metal chain outside the jar to allow the electrical charge to pass into the jar. Nollet asked the soldiers to stand in an open circle and hold hands. When he told them to, the first and last soldier each touched the jar, completing the circle. The electricity passed through each soldier at the same time with the result that all 180 soldiers jumped into the air simultaneously. The king was highly amused by this and made Nollet repeat the demonstration using priests. Nollet did many other demonstrations and experiments and news of his work spread throughout the scientific community.

I had decided not to go to university to study when I left school. At this stage I had not yet started doing my own experiments and I really wanted to learn as much as I could from Nollet. He later became the first Professor of Experimental Physics at the University of Paris. I was also in contact with Professor Giovanni Battista Beccaria of the University of Turin and I sent him a paper I wrote in Latin called *On the attractive force of electric fire*. Later, in 1769, it was published. I started doing my own experiments. This was a slow process and I made many mistakes. I also learnt a great deal and in 1774, when I was 29, I became Professor of Physics at the Royal School in Como.

♦ ♦ ♦

Ten years previously, a Swedish physicist called Johan Wilcke had invented a generator which produced static electricity. In 1775, I invented an improved version of his generator, called the electrophorus. My invention was more useful because it was able to produce a larger amount of static electricity and to produce it continuously. Later it was developed so that it could store electricity.

In 1777, I went to Switzerland and met with a physicist and geologist called H. B. de Saussure, who helped me develop my ideas and I continued my research. I was looking at atmospheric electricity and at the instruments Saussure had developed to measure it. I was able to alter his instruments to make them more accurate so that electrical tension, as it was known, could be measured. In 1881, many years after my death, the unit of measurement was named the 'volt' in my honour. As more people in the science community noticed my work, more opportunities became available to me.

The next year, my attention turned to the chemistry of gases and in 1778, I discovered a dangerous gas which was later called methane. One day when I was on holiday, in a boat on a lake, I saw some bubbles coming up through the water. The air above the bubbles smelt horrible and naturally I was curious to discover what it was. I managed to get some of the bad-smelling air back to my laboratory and found that it was inflammable – that is, that it burnt easily. As the gas had come from beneath the ground, I continued my research. It was discovered that methane was a gas that was present in mines, and because of its inflammable nature it was extremely dangerous.

♦ ♦ ♦

In 1779, I moved to Pavia in northern Italy where I became Professor of Experimental Physics at the university. Six years later I became Rector – the head – of the university but I continued to do research. Electricity was still the subject I thought most about. Each summer in our region there were giant thunderstorms. I was fascinated by the noise of thunder and <u>sparks</u> of lightning and wondered if we could capture the power I was seeing and use it. Meanwhile, I started looking at frogs.

In 1791, an Italian physicist and medical doctor called Luigi Galvani had been working on a theory he called animal electricity. He noticed one day while working in his laboratory that the leg of the dead frog he was examining moved when it was touched by a spark of static electricity from a metal instrument. The frog's leg itself gave off tiny sparks of static and it jumped as if it was alive. Galvani suggested that it was the liquid in the frog's leg that carried an electric current. I repeated Galvani's experiments myself and at first I thought his suggestion was correct. However, as I looked more closely and did more experiments, I decided that he had been wrong. It wasn't the frog's leg that was conducting the electricity – allowing the electricity to pass through it – but the metal that Galvani had been using to connect parts of the frog. My future work on batteries would confirm my <u>findings</u>.

In 1794, I received the Copley Medal from the Royal Society of London for my work on Galvani's original research. 1794 was also the year I got married. I was nearly fifty when I met a young woman called Teresa Peregrini, who was the youngest of seven daughters. Her father was a wealthy man from my hometown of Como. Teresa's father would not let her get married until her six sisters had got married. She was much younger than me but it didn't matter and after she was finally allowed to marry me, we started our family. Sadly, only two of our three sons survived to adulthood.

In 1799, I discovered the electro-chemical series, which measures how reactive different chemicals are – that is, how each chemical behaves when it comes into contact with other chemicals – and I continued experimenting. One day later that year, we had dramatic results when I created what was called the Voltaic Pile. I combined copper, zinc and cardboard with salt water which I placed on top of them. Then I attached a piece of wire to the top and bottom, through which an electric current would pass, if the ends of the wires were touching. It would become the first electric battery.

The following year, I made the first working battery, which produced a steady stream of electricity, by again connecting copper and zinc with a wire. I sent my findings to Sir Joseph Banks at the Royal Society of London, making my results available for other scientists to work on. Among others, William Nicholson and Humphry Davy developed the Voltaic Pile battery further and until the first electric generator was invented by Michael Faraday in 1870, the whole of the nineteenth century electrical industry was powered by battery.

◆ ◆ ◆

In November 1801, I went to France and gave three lectures at the Institut National de France, which Napoleon Bonaparte himself attended. I was made a member of the Institute, one of only eight foreigners. In 1805, Napoleon honoured me with the *Légion d'honneur* and, to my surprise,

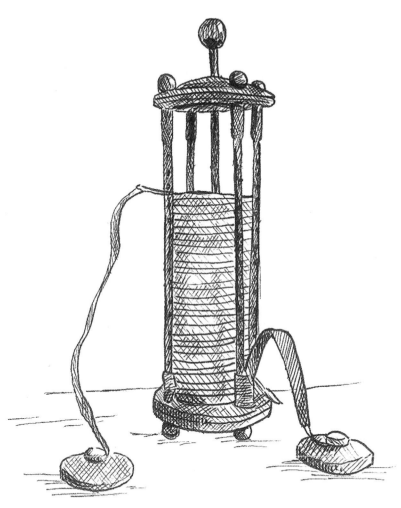

A Voltaic Pile – the first electric battery

The Volta Temple, Como

also gave me a considerable amount of money in <u>recognition</u> of my work. In 1806, I was also honoured in my own country, when I received the Cavalier of the Italian Royal Order of the Iron Crown. Then in 1809, I became a Senator of the Kingdom of Italy. In 1810, Napoleon gave me a title, Count Alessandro Giuseppe Antonio Anastasio, a high honour indeed for a self-taught scientist.

Outside of work, I lived a relatively quiet life and in 1813, I moved on from lecturing. My aim was to continue the search to advance the understanding and application of physics. In addition, I wanted to help the new generation of <u>innovators</u> to do further research into electrochemistry. I was made Professor of Philosophy at Padua University in 1815. By the time I was 74, in 1819, my health was not good and I decided it was time I retired.

In 1827 when I was 82, I died at my home in Como surrounded by my family – my wife and our two sons. At the time of my death, there were many young men who followed on from me: Michael Faraday, 28 years of age, George Ohm, 30 years old and Joseph Henry who was 22 years of age, are just a few of them. I never met these new inventors but their discoveries, and the knowledge of electricity they <u>inherited</u> from scientists of my generation, were the <u>foundation</u> for the Industrial Revolution.

The Life of Alessandro Volta

1745   Alessandro Giuseppe Antonio Anastasio
        Volta was born on 18th February in Como,
        Italy.

1752   Alessandro's father died.

1760   He enrolled in the school in Como to study
        natural philosophy. Alessandro also studied
        many languages including Latin, French,
        English, Dutch, Spanish, Russian and
        Greek.

1763   Alessandro was interested in physics and
        chemistry. He began to write to the Abbé
        Jean-Antoine Nollet, in Paris, and later to
        Professor Giovanni Battista Beccaria, at
        the University of Turin, on the subject of
        electricity.

1769   He published *De vi attractive ignis electrici (On
        the attractive force of electric fire)*.

1774   Alessandro was appointed Director and
        then Professor of Physics at the Royal
        School, Como, Italy. The following
        year, he improved an invention that
        produced a static electric charge called the
        electrophorus.

1776–1778   Alessandro focused his study on the
             chemistry of gases. He discovered methane.
             He also studied electrical potential and
             charge, from which the Volta Lamp was
             developed.

1779   He became Professor of Experimental
             Physics at the University of Pavia.
             Alessandro also travelled to Switzerland,
             which was the first of many trips.

1781   Alessandro lectured throughout
             Switzerland, Belgium, Germany, Holland,
             France and England.

1783   He travelled to Vienna and met with
             Emperor Joseph II.

1785   Alessandro became the Rector at the
             University of Pavia.

1791   Luigi Galvani's reports on experiments
             with 'animal electricity' were published.
             Alessandro carried out experiments of
             his own, which led to his theory that
             animal tissue was not required to conduct
             electricity. This would later be proven by
             his development of the battery.

1794   Alessandro was awarded the Copley Medal
        by the Royal Society of London for his
        work in chemistry. Alessandro married
        Teresa Peregrini, who came from a wealthy
        family in Como. They later had three sons,
        one of whom died aged 18.

1799   After completing his own experiments,
        Alessandro disagreed with the findings
        of Luigi Galvani. He developed the first
        electric battery, known as the Voltaic
        Pile. Alessandro also discovered the law of
        electromotive forces.

1800   He wrote to Sir Joseph Banks of the Royal
        Society of London and described his
        findings. That led to further experiments
        and development in electricity and batteries.

1801   Alessandro travelled to Paris and lectured at
        the Institut National de France.

1805–1809   He was created a Knight of the Legion of
        Honour, Knight of the Iron Crown and
        Senator of the Realm.

1810   Napoleon Bonaparte granted Alessandro
        the title of Count, to honour his work in
        the field of electricity.

1813   Alessandro stopped teaching.

1846 The following year, the Royal Society awarded him the Rumford Medal in recognition of his scientific work.

1815 The Emperor of Austria named Alessandro Professor of Philosophy at the University of Padua. Later, many of his works were published in Florence.

1819 He retired to his estate in Como, Italy.

1827 Alessandro died aged 82, in Como, Italy. The important electrical unit, the volt, was named in Alessandro's honour in 1881.

Michael Faraday

◆ ◆

1791–1867

the man who invented the electric motor

I learned only basic reading, writing and <u>arithmetic</u>. But I changed the future of the world by discovering that electricity could be made by using <u>magnets</u>.

◆ ◆ ◆

I was born on 22nd September 1791. My family lived in Newington Butts, which was a village close to London. My parents had nine children, but as was not unusual, only four survived. My father, who was a <u>blacksmith</u>, couldn't work properly because he had health problems and as a result, we were a family that was always fighting poverty. London was an overcrowded dirty city and the streets were full of disease and dirt. Unless you were rich, there was almost no medical help and our living facilities, like those of all poor people, were basic. When it rained or snowed, <u>damp</u> covered everything and the city was permanently covered in smoke from the fires that every house burned.

It was not only money and health care that was lacking, but also a formal education. I was lucky enough to go to school, at least for long enough to learn the basics of writing and counting, but it was the Sunday School at the local church which helped me most. We would read the Bible, sing and <u>pray</u> – all of which were good for disciplining the mind. Childhood ends early when you're poor and when I was 13, it was time for me to start earning my living. There was a bookshop in Jacob Well Mews near our home that was owned by a Frenchman called Mr Riebau. He offered me a job as an errand boy – running around doing jobs and making deliveries – and I met a lot of interesting people.

After a year, Mr Riebau offered to teach me <u>bookbinding</u> and that was the start of my seven-year <u>apprenticeship</u>. While I was waiting for customers, there was plenty of time to read the books in the shop, particularly the ones on science. Mr Riebau encouraged me to read *Conversations on Chemistry* and I also had access to the *Encyclopedia Britannica*. Most of our customers were educated people and some helped me, like the French artist who taught me how to draw. It was something that would prove valuable in my later work. Even though I had been brought up in a very religious family, I soon began to understand that science would provide the answers to the problems we were all facing rather than religion. However, the transition from believing in the importance of religion to believing in the importance of science was not an easy one for me. So my religious background stayed with me my whole life.

One day Mr Riebau told me that a lecturer called Mr Tatum was giving four talks on the subject of <u>natural</u>

philosophy, and that I should go. My elder brother, Robert, had given me a shilling – there were twenty shillings in a pound – and I used it to pay to go to the talks. I met people, some who became friends and others who were useful to me professionally and I tried to remember everything that Mr Tatum said. A shilling was a lot to spend to listen to someone talking. However, it was the best shilling I ever spent because those lectures changed my life.

◆ ◆ ◆

The years passed and I was now 21. I had finished my bookbinding training and I was keen to learn more about science. I went to hear four more lectures, this time given by Sir Humphry Davy, who was a chemist, and I was completely fascinated. Many mysteries of science were explained in the lectures but a large number of questions still remained unanswered. I had made so many notes throughout the years, while I was reading in the shop and from the previous lectures I had been to, that I decided to make a book with them. Using my skills in bookbinding, I made a 300-page leather-bound book. I sent one copy to Sir Joseph Banks, who was famous as the botanist who had travelled with the great explorer, Captain Cook, but, to my great disappointment, he didn't even reply. This didn't stop me, however, and I sent another copy to Sir Humphry Davy.

This time my efforts were successful and Sir Humphry Davy invited me to meet him. Our meeting went well and he gave me a temporary job as his assistant. This was an amazing opportunity for me to learn about exciting experiments. Some of them were quite risky, as they could be dangerous but it was the start of great new adventures. The next year, Sir Humphry Davy asked me to go with him on a lecture tour of Europe. At that time, Emperor Napoleon was the ruler in France. He did not like the English, but luckily for us, he liked Sir Humphry Davy. Sir Humphry's great work on chemistry was recognized in France and Napoleon provided us with documents that allowed us to travel around Europe safely.

We toured France, Italy, Switzerland, Germany and Holland, spending 18 months on rough roads, travelling through wind, rain and sun. It was my job to write down everything that was said in the lectures and it proved to be the kind of education that one cannot get from books. As well as seeing many countries and meeting such a wide variety of people, I also met some <u>influential</u> people who would be able to help me in the future. My head was full of the knowledge I gained about science, culture, language, history, geography and of course, life. On our return to London, I knew I had a lot to do.

I met many new friends and, growing in confidence, I gave my first lecture in 1816. This was the start of a new age as the European wars came to an end and we celebrated our victory at the Battle of Waterloo on 18th June 1815 when Napoleon's army was defeated. I had met many beautiful young women in the countries we visited, but I met my future wife after I returned home. Her name was Sarah Barnard and we met at the church I regularly went to. We got married on 2nd June 1821. Happy at home, my energies went back into my work and I started a long career in science.

◆ ◆ ◆

For the next 45 years, I researched and taught at the Royal Institution, all the while making sure I followed all the new developments at home and overseas. In Denmark, it was found that an electric current created a magnetic field – an area in which the push and pull of a magnet can be felt, and electro-magnetism was born. I wondered if the reverse could be true. Was it possible that electricity could be created from magnetism? In the next few months, I worked on building an electric motor. It was a very basic system with a magnet, a chemical battery and some wire. When the current flowed, the wire turned the magnet round. Many thought the idea was just for fun and couldn't see how it could be used; Sir Humphry Davy seemed annoyed and claimed the idea was his, but to me it was just one of many experiments.

By 1823, my reputation as a scientist was rising as I managed to turn the chemical <u>element</u> <u>chlorine</u> into liquid, and discovered the chemical <u>compound</u> <u>benzene</u>. In 1824, I was elected to the Royal Society – sadly, the only person who objected to this was Sir Humphry Davy. Remembering how as a young man, attending my first lectures had changed my life, I started the Christmas Lectures and I helped to provide electricity for <u>lighthouses</u>, which saved countless lives at sea. Between 1830 and 1851, I was also Professor of Chemistry and spent time giving lectures at the Royal Military Academy in Woolwich in London.

I was busy doing many experiments and it seemed likely that I was about to make a big breakthrough. I did. On

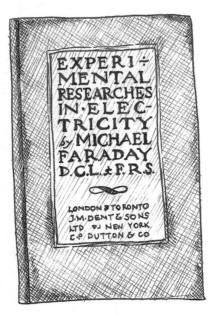

Volume one of *Experimental Researches in Electricity*

29th August 1831, I was able to give a demonstration as to how an electric transformer worked. A transformer was a piece of equipment that changed one kind of electrical force to another. The following month there was another success. The principle of electro–magnetic induction became clear to me: two wires were attached to a copper disc, which was turned round in a horseshoe magnet. It sounds simple, but it was the first electric generator, leading to the invention of direct electric current. This literally lit up the world and led the way for the creation of an alternative power to steam.

It was a time of high creativity and it was as if the secrets of the heavens were being opened for me to see. In 1833, a sponsor, Mr Fuller, provided money for research and as a result, I became the Fullerian Professor of Chemistry at the Royal Institution of Great Britain. Other work led to the creation of important laws and a whole new language was required to explain the new developments. Words like 'cathode' and 'electrode' and 'ion' had to be defined and dictionaries had to explain terms like electro-magnetism and transformers.

Politicians and businessmen asked my views on social and business issues and the British Government asked me to serve on committees. Each one was a major project, whether it was industrial pollution in Swansea in Wales, air pollution in London, or <u>sewage</u> and the very bad smell from the River Thames, also in London. All of them were terrible problems because of their effects on people's lives and health.

There were pleasanter projects when I worked on the Great Exhibition of 1851 and helped the National Gallery to protect their art collection. I met many people who invited me to work on other projects and time flew by. The problem was that I had less time to contribute to science, so I focused on writing the book *Chemical Manipulation*, my scientific articles and a regular diary. The work was demanding and exciting, but then I began to feel unwell. Worry and stress took over my life so much that I became ill with a nervous breakdown. It was six years before I could focus on work again.

When I did return, I invented what was called the Faraday Effect. I looked at the impact of magnetic fields on <u>light waves</u>, which convinced me there was a single universal force. My religious beliefs were still very important to me, but there was no scientific proof of the single force. Was it a force of God or of Nature, or both? How did it operate? I wanted desperately to think about these issues but once again my health prevented further efforts and I became confused and anxious. At the age of 64, I started to suffer from senility – a condition that makes old people confused and behave in a strange way.

Queen Victoria, who was the queen of Britain from 1837 until 1901, was kind and offered me a cottage at one of the royal palaces, Hampton Court. She also offered me a knighthood, which I turned down, preferring to remain just plain Michael Faraday. I didn't need the title 'Sir' – seeing my work recognized was enough of a reward. I never saw electric lights in homes and electric power in medicine and business because in 1867 I died. However, I had been so fascinated by chemistry, physics and electronics and the power they held, that I was sure technology in the future would be far greater than I could ever dream about.

The Life of Michael Faraday

1791   Michael Faraday was born on 22nd September in Newington Butts, England, to a relatively poor family. His father was a blacksmith, and his mother a housewife.

1795   The family moved to rooms on the western edge of London.

1804   Michael learned basic reading, writing and arithmetic at a local school.

1805   Michael was employed at a bookshop, by George Riebau, as an apprentice bookbinder for seven years. During that time, he developed an interest in science.

1809   He started to record his readings and experiments in *Philosophical Miscellany*. His father died the same year.

1812   At the age of 21, Michael attended lectures by English chemist, Sir Humphry Davy.

1813–1815   He was employed as a laboratory assistant to Sir Humphry Davy at the Royal Institution. Michael travelled with Sir Humphry, as his assistant, on a science tour of Europe.

1818–1822   He began a project to improve the quality of steel alloys – metals that were a mixture of at least two other metals.

1821   Michael was appointed as Superintendent of the House of the Royal Institution. He married Sarah Barnard. The couple did not have any children.

1823   He turned gas into a liquid form for the first time.

1824–1825   Michael was elected Fellow of the Royal Society. The following year, he became the director of the laboratory at the Royal Institution.

1827   He published *Chemical Manipulation*.

1831   Michael invented the electro-magnetic generator.

1832   He received an <u>honorary</u> <u>doctorate</u> from Oxford University. In the same year, he established the laws of electrolysis and received the Copley Medal, which was awarded by the Royal Society of London. He received a second Copley Medal six years later.

1833   He was appointed first Fullerian Professor of Chemistry at the Royal Institution.

1835   Michael was awarded a pension by Queen Victoria. He also received a Royal Medal from the Royal Society. He was awarded a second medal, in 1846.

1836 He became Scientific Adviser to Trinity House, which was the official authority for lighthouses.

1838 Michael's mother died. He was elected to the Swedish Academy of Sciences. A year later, he published Volume one of *Experimental Researches in Electricity*.

1844 Volume two of *Experimental Researches in Electricity* was published. Michael was elected to the French Academy of Sciences.

1846 The following year, the Royal Society awarded him the Rumford Medal in recognition of his scientific work.

1849 He worked on the relations between <u>gravity</u> and electricity.

1855 Volume three of *Experimental Researches in Electricity* was published.

1859 *Experimental Researches in Chemistry and Physics* was published.

1863 Michael received an honorary doctorate from Cambridge University.

1867 Michael died, just before his 76th birthday, at Hampton Court, Middlesex, England.

Marie Curie

◆ ◆ ◆

1867–1934

the first person to be awarded two Nobel Prizes

As a scientist, I don't think I could have had a more rewarding life. As a female scientist, my professional achievements were unbelievable. I was the first woman to become a professor at the Sorbonne and the first woman to receive a Nobel Prize.

◆ ◆ ◆

When I was born in 1867, my parents registered me as Maria Salomea Sklodowska, but I am now better known as Marie Curie. I was their last child, one of five, born at the Freta Street Boarding School, where my mother was principal. The apartment we lived in was part of my mother's salary. We lived in Warsaw, Poland, which was at that time <u>occupied</u> by the Russians. My mother was a musician and my father was a mathematician who had lost his job as a teacher. As a result we were poor and had to rent out rooms to make enough money. My parents loved their country and wanted it to be free from occupation.

When I was twelve years old my mother died of tuberculosis, a nasty disease that affected the lungs and other organs of the body. There was no cure and as I watched her slowly die, I started to think about whether I could do anything to help other people with the same illness. I had a cousin who ran the Museum of Industry and Agriculture in Warsaw and he encouraged my interest in science. In Poland, access to university science education was available only to men. Instead, women had a secret, illegal organization, a 'floating university', which was a network of people who taught each other. We moved from one house to another and shared our knowledge. My cousin let me do some practical scientific training and experiments at the museum, but to progress any further, it was necessary to go to another country and study there. This was an ambition I shared with my sister Bronislawa. Others might have called it a dream, but we found a way to make it really happen.

Actually, it was quite a simple plan. I would stay in Poland and work while Bronislawa would study abroad, supported by the money I was earning. When she had finished her education and had found a job, it would be my turn to study while she supported me. We put the first part of our plan into action when Bronislawa left Poland to study in Paris. For my first job, I lived with a lawyer's family in Kraków, teaching the children, and then I went to another family in Ciechanów, where I stayed for two years. I met the son of the family and we fell in love. We wanted to get married but I was a poor girl and his family disapproved of me so we had to break up. I was unhappy after this and needed to get away and I moved to Sopot, in the north of Poland. Here

I lived with yet another family for a year, working by day and studying by night. In the meantime, my sister had got married and was now in a position where she could help me financially. She invited me to come and stay with her, so at the age of 24, I went to Paris.

♦ ♦ ♦

I stayed with Bronislawa for a while and then rented a little room of my own, right at the top of a house. It wasn't comfortable or warm but I felt a sense of freedom that I had never had before. I managed to become a student at the Sorbonne University and I would study during the day and work as a tutor in the evening. I got my Master's degree in physics and then a year later I also got a degree in mathematics. Living in a foreign country wasn't easy, especially studying in a foreign language, but I was determined to succeed. Despite my sister's help, I had very little money and sometimes I survived on just bread and tea with the result that I was often unwell. However, I was achieving my ambition, and that was more important to me than my health.

From the beginning, I was interested in magnetism – the force that makes two objects pull towards or away from each other. In 1894, I was offered a job studying the energy in <u>iron ore</u> to see what <u>magnetic</u> powers it had, and needed a laboratory to work in. A friend introduced me to a quiet, rather shy man, another scientist, who had the kind of space I needed. He encouraged me and soon we felt a special connection of our own, for magnetism also applies to people. This kind man was, of course, Pierre Curie, who was to become my husband. At the time, he was an instructor at the School of Physics and Chemistry, and in 1900 became Professor of General Physics at the Sorbonne. My task was to try to <u>isolate</u> <u>radioactive</u> material in the iron ore. This involved <u>melting</u> iron in a huge container. It was hard work and the conditions were less than perfect as I was either outside or in a rough kind of shed. I didn't know it at the time, but this was fortunate as the melting iron gave off a poisonous gas that probably would have done me a lot of harm if I had been indoors. Much later, in the 1930s, it was also discovered that people exposed to <u>radiation</u> were at risk of developing anaemia – a disease of the blood – and bone cancer.

Pierre and I would spend endless hours discussing our research and our friendship became more and more serious as time passed. We decided to get engaged and then we got married in 1895. I felt incredibly lucky. Not only had I found a good man to share my home life with but I also had someone who shared my love of science. I was no longer alone. Two years later, I got my <u>Doctorate</u> in Physics – I was the first woman in France to do this – and then a second special event happened when our daughter Irène was born in the same year.

In the meantime, with our joint energy and ideas, we were taking science into completely new areas. I was interested in the work of Henri Becquerel – a scientist at the French Academy of Sciences – on a heavy white metal called uranium. He discovered that uranium gave off <u>rays</u> that were similar to, but weaker than, the X-rays Wilhelm Roentgen, a German scientist, had just discovered. Continuing

Becquerel's research, I found that rays from the uranium stayed the same no matter what condition or form the metal was in. To me this meant only one thing – that the rays had come from the atomic structure of the uranium – and that meant that we had discovered what I called radioactivity. I saw radioactivity as being an amazing gift from nature. We needed to capture its power and control it.

Our studies built on this aim through further research. The <u>mineral</u> we now started to study, called pitchblende, may not sound very exciting, but what we found would change the future. We discovered two new radioactive <u>elements,</u> one that I called polonium after my beloved Poland and the other, radium. This was truly magical material, but what could we do with it? We continued experimenting and found that it was very effective on human skin problems, for example, radium could burn off cancers. Doctors started using it as a treatment and it quickly became known as 'Curie therapy'.

♦ ◆ ♦

I continued working with my husband and we found out how to isolate pure radium. In 1903, this earned us and Becquerel a Nobel Prize. We used the money to pay for more research and to support poor science students who otherwise would not have been able to continue their studies. With the birth of our second daughter, Eve, in 1904, it looked as if we could successfully combine both our family and professional lives. Then, in 1906, the unthinkable happened. Pierre accidentally stepped in front of a horse and was killed. I was now a single mother with two children. I was heartbroken and didn't know how I was going to continue without him.

The Sorbonne offered me my husband's position at the university, making me the first ever woman professor there. I continued doing Pierre's work and my own, but was ignored by the French Science Academy. I had the feeling that they did not like the fact that I was both female and Polish. These two things seemed more important to them than the scientific discoveries I made. In addition, people in the scientific community talked about me, which I'm sure also harmed my professional reputation. For a long time after Pierre's death, I was in shock and I tried to balance work and family life. Through my work, I got to know Paul Langevin, who had been a student of Pierre's. In my darkest days after Pierre's death, his support helped me to get through and we gradually became friends. His marriage was in difficulty and in 1910 it ended. People in the scientific community knew about our friendship and blamed me for the break-up. It was surprising that this happened in Paris, where people were not usually blamed for problems in their personal lives.

My personal life may have affected how seriously my work was seen by some people at home in France, but it didn't stop me from receiving a second Nobel Prize in 1911. This time it was for chemistry, for having measured the atomic weight of radium. I was the first person to have been given the Nobel Prize twice. My work on radioactivity and X-rays continued and during the First World War we saw the terrible effects the bombing and shooting were having on French and British soldiers. With my daughter Irène,

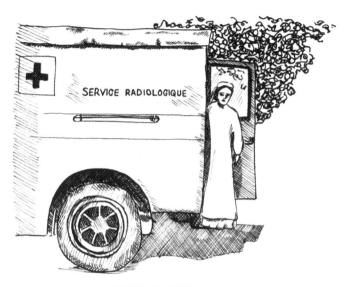

A 'Little Curie' X-ray van

I set up X-ray vans that could travel round to all the field hospitals – the temporary hospitals that were near where soldiers were fighting – and we trained 150 radiographers to use them to assess serious injuries. The vans soon got their own name – 'Little Curies'.

◆ ◆ ◆

After the war, <u>recognition</u> for my work came from the USA and I started travelling widely to encourage other scientists. It was very important to try and get as many people as possible to continue making advances with radiotherapy treatments. The new technology could cure illness, help reduce pain and suffering, and extend people's lives. We had already set up the Radium Institute in Paris in 1919 and in 1925 my sister Bronislawa opened another branch in

The Radium Institute, Warsaw

Warsaw, becoming its director. My daughter, Irène, now also a scientist, won the Nobel Prize in 1935 for inventing artificial radioactivity. It was an achievement that her father would have been proud of.

However, I had been working all my adult life with dangerous radioactive materials, so it was not surprising when in 1934 I became seriously unwell. I was diagnosed with the type of anaemia that can be caused by long-term <u>exposure</u> to radiation and at the age of 66, I died.

In the course of my life I had been a sister, wife, mother, student, scientist, teacher and technical specialist, as well as working in managerial roles. I had done many things that had never been done before by a woman and I considered my life more than worthwhile.

The Life of Marie Curie

1867   Marie was born on 7th November in
        Warsaw, Poland, then part of the Russian
        <u>empire</u>. She was named Maria Salomea
        Sklodowska.

1877   Marie's eldest sister, Zofia, died. Marie
        attended a boarding school and then a high
        school for girls.

1879   Her mother died when Marie was 12.

1883   She graduated from the high school. The
        following year, she lived in the countryside
        with relatives, before returning to work in
        Warsaw as a tutor.

1885   Around this time, she studied at the
        Floating University, in Warsaw, which was
        an underground educational institution
        for those not able to gain education in the
        official organizations. In the years that
        followed, Marie agreed to financially support
        her sister while she was studying in Paris. In
        the meantime, Marie worked as a governess
        in Poland, while keeping her promise and
        supporting her sister. She fell in love with
        Kazimierz Zorawski, the son of the family
        where she worked as a governess. His parents
        did not support their relationship, and she
        moved to another part of Poland.

1890   Marie returned to Warsaw and tutored at the Floating University and then began her scientific training in a laboratory at the Museum of Industry and Agriculture.

1891   At the age of 24, she followed her older sister, Bronislawa, who was working as a doctor, to Paris. Marie studied physics, chemistry and mathematics at the Sorbonne University.

1893   She was awarded a degree in physics from the Sorbonne. Marie began working in an industrial laboratory.

1894   She earned her degree in mathematics from the Sorbonne. She met Pierre Curie.

1895   Marie and Pierre Curie got married. They shared many interests including laboratory experiments.

1896   Henri Becquerel discovered radioactivity, which inspired Marie and Pierre to carry out further research.

1897   She gave birth to their first daughter, Irène, and taught her the Polish language.

1898   Marie and her husband, Pierre, discovered two new elements. One of them they called polonium, after her native Poland. The other element was called radium.

1900   Marie became the first woman to be a staff member of the Ecole Normale Supérieure in Paris.

1903   She gained her Doctor of Science degree from the Sorbonne. The Royal Swedish Academy of Sciences awarded Marie, Pierre Curie and Henri Becquerel the Nobel Prize for Physics. Marie became the first woman to win a Nobel Prize.

1904   Their second daughter, Eve, was born. After her mother's death, Eve later wrote a famous biography of her mother, published in 1937, called *Madame Curie*. Marie published *Investigations on Radioactive Substances*.

1906   Tragically, Pierre died in a street accident. Marie was offered his position as Professor of General Physics in the Faculty of Sciences at the Sorbonne and became the first woman to become a professor at the Sorbonne.

1910   Marie published *Treatise on Radioactivity*.

1911   The Royal Swedish Academy of Sciences awarded Marie a second Nobel Prize for Chemistry. She then became the first woman to win two Nobel Prizes.

1914–1918   Marie was the first person to use mobile radiography units, known as *petites Curies* (little Curies). They contained X-ray equipment and were used on the battle-fields to assist in the treatment of wounded soldiers.

1920   The Curie Foundation was established.

1921   Marie was presented with one gram of radium, in recognition of her contribution to science, by President Harding of the United States, and on behalf of the women of America.

1924   Marie published a biography of her husband, Pierre Curie.

1925   She founded the Warsaw Radium Institute.

1929   President Hoover of the United States presented her with a large sum of money, which was donated by the American Friends of Science to purchase radium to be used in the laboratory in Warsaw.

1930   Marie's discovery of radium was developed
        and applications were used in aircraft
        switches, clocks and instrument dials.
        During the 1930s, it was also discovered
        that people exposed to radiation were at
        risk of serious health problems, including
        anaemia and bone cancer.

1934   Marie died, aged 66, in Passy, Haute-
        Savoie, France. She died from anaemia,
        after being exposed for too long a period
        to radiation, when working unprotected
        with radioactive materials. A year after
        her death, her daughter Irène and her
        husband, Frédéric, also won a Nobel Prize
        for Chemistry, for the discovery of artificial
        radioactivity.

Albert Einstein

◆ ◆ ◆

1879–1955

the man who was responsible for the
Theory of Relativity

**The release of atomic power has changed everything
except our way of thinking ... the solution to this problem
lies in the heart of mankind. If only I had known, I would
have become a watchmaker.**

◆ ◆ ◆

I was born on 4th March 1876 in Ulm, Germany, and two
years later we moved to Munich. When I was five years old
my parents gave me a compass. I was already interested in
travel and wanted to explore. But unlike others who thought
about touring from one country to another, what I wanted
was to discover other galaxies. The compass was to me what
a teddy bear might have been to another child and I always
carried it with me.

I was a child who did not speak very much. This worried
my parents, especially my father. He was a salesman with a
natural talent with words and did not understand why I was

not like him. But I was more <u>introverted</u> than my parents and I preferred my own company to that of others. I would sit by myself for hours and read books, many books. My parents also thought it was important to be well-educated. I, however, did things my own way and when I was about ten, I started to plan my own education. Science was at the very top of my list.

Every week, my parents would invite Max Talmey, a poor medical student from Poland, to lunch. He introduced me to books on science and mathematics. Experiments in physics and chemistry fascinated me, and to me, mathematics was a beautiful language. At school we had to learn things by heart, which made it all so boring and we were punished if we didn't remember everything the teachers told us. I knew there had to be a better way of learning than that.

◆ ◆ ◆

In 1891, when I was fifteen years old, we moved to Pavia, Italy. I now had to learn a new language and I knew that sitting in a classroom was not the way to do it. I learnt Italian by meeting people, talking in cafés and doing little jobs. I wanted to learn about technical subjects but I didn't have good enough grades to get into the local school. Instead, I went to Aarau in Switzerland to finish high school and then I enrolled at the Federal Polytechnic in Zurich. That year I gave up my German citizenship and for the next few years I did not 'belong' to any country. I had been born into a Jewish family but I didn't like the rules that religion forced people to follow. I couldn't see why we had to lead the lives chosen for us by our parents, so I gave up Judaism.

At college, I noticed an attractive girl called Mileva Maric, who had just arrived from Serbia. She had some problems in speaking Swiss German, which I was able to help her with, and we also studied together. We became close friends. At the age of twenty-two, I decided to apply for, and was given Swiss citizenship. I was supposed to do my military service but because of a few physical problems, which were not serious, I was excused. This suited me extremely well as thoughts were more important to me than physical action. I returned to Italy for a while to stay with my parents and Mileva came with me. My parents welcomed her as part of the family and we lived with them.

I wanted to become a physics teacher but did not have the necessary qualifications so I applied to be a patent examiner instead. A patent is a document that gives you the right to make or sell a new invention. I was given a job by the Swiss Patent Office. This meant I now had a steady income and could set up a home in Bern, so I asked Mileva to marry me. Being married was the start of a new way of life for me and within a year, our son Hans Albert was born. My home life, work and research were all moving fast.

After work, in the evening, I would study physics and always discussed my ideas with my friend Michele Besso. He was an excellent listener, asking questions that really made me think deeply. We started our own organization called the Olympia Academy – we had to because nobody else would take us seriously. There was no money for me to set up a laboratory, so I studied research that had already been published and then <u>coordinated</u> all the results. This actually suited me because I believed that evidence was better than opinion. Since I was no better with words now than when I was a child, I preferred something that was both solid and abstract. Words had many different meanings and <u>interpretations</u> but symbols were real to me.

It was obvious that we were part of a universe that was beyond words. How could we describe what we could not see? How could we see what we could not measure? Yet it was quite clear that we were influenced by these unseen forces. Our tides moved with the moon and our earth with the sun. Beyond that there was the cosmos – the universe – working to its own timetable. I was working on the relationship between time, space and movement, which later became known as the theory of relativity. I wrote four papers about it – one of which was published in a leading German physics publication. Then, at the age of twenty-six, I proposed the equation $e=mc^2$. This meant that if you measured the <u>mass</u> of any object and <u>multiplied</u> it by the speed of light, you discovered the amount of energy it could produce. Previously, scientists had thought that there was no relation between mass and energy.

The response, as I expected, was huge, with a great deal of discussion taking place. Before long, professors at various universities wanted to meet me. To me it was amazing that my work should be recognized, considering that I had been an average student and had never really followed a formal system of education. However, studying mainly by myself had its advantages. I was able to think in a wider way, allowing me to form my theories. Academic job offers started coming in and I worked for a time in Zurich. At

$$\varepsilon = mc^2$$

home, we celebrated the birth of our second son, Eduard, but unfortunately our marriage was not going well.

I did some of my best work at night. I would watch the stars and see the sun rise and it seemed that the light from the stars was bending towards the sun. I published my findings in 1911 but not many people believed what I was suggesting. My tutors at Zurich did recognize the research, however, and later that year I became a full professor – the most senior type of professor – at the German University in Prague and was also given a job at the Prussian Academy of Science in Berlin.

Mileva didn't want to live in Berlin and so I went there on my own. I shared a house with my cousin, Elsa Loewenthal. Elsa was very interested in my work and we became close friends. Mileva was not happy about this relationship and when she eventually came to Berlin, it was obvious that our marriage was over. Mileva took our sons and left. After a two-year separation that was full of bitter disagreements, we decided to get divorced. In the meantime, the First World War had started but I was able to continue with my research work and I published *On the General Theory of Relativity*.

Before the divorce became final, Mileva had heard that I might win a Nobel Prize. She insisted that she would get the prize money so that she wouldn't have to worry about how she and our sons were going to survive. Naturally I agreed, but I found this whole period extremely stressful and I was not at all well. Elsa nursed me through my illness and once I had recovered, we decided to get married.

Then, in 1919, a chance to test my theory of relativity happened when there was an <u>eclipse</u> of the sun. My ideas were supported and those of Newton's were questioned. During that time, my work on cosmology – the study of how the universe was made – was published. Invitations came flooding in from all over the world as people wanted to hear my views. In 1922, the Nobel Prize for Physics was awarded to me. The cash prize, as agreed, was sent to Mileva, who bought some property with it. My work continued and the Einstein Institute in Potsdam was opened in 1924. I was interested in learning more about quantum mechanics, which is the study of atoms – these are the smallest parts of an <u>element</u> – and working with Niels Bohr, significant advances were made.

After several years of travelling and working non-stop, I started to feel unwell again. Doctors said it was mental stress that was making me feel ill. The <u>Great Depression</u> brought poverty and <u>despair</u> to many and money for research was more difficult to find. Added to that was the rise of <u>Nazism</u> in Germany. In particular, Jews were under attack and I could not work there. I may have given up my religion but on paper I was still Jewish, so we made arrangements for me to take a job in the USA. Elsa and I arrived there in 1933 and I started work at the Institute for Advanced Study in Princeton. Soon, I noticed that Elsa was not very well. The doctors were unable to help her and in 1936 she died. More sad news was coming from Germany, where many Jews had already been killed.

In the meantime, scientists had been able to split the atom and it was recognized that the results – tiny pieces of radioactive material – had the potential to release huge amounts of nuclear energy in the form of a new deadly weapon – the atom bomb. In 1939, a friend of mine, Leo Szilard, who was a Hungarian physicist, wrote to President Roosevelt in the USA with the horrible warning that Germany might be making this new weapon. He wrote that for its own protection the USA ought to start work immediately and make an American atomic bomb. Szilard was not well-known outside the scientific community and President Roosevelt did not take him seriously. Leo asked me to write as well, and this time the President took notice of what we were saying. As a result, a top-secret research programme called the Manhattan Project was started, in a hurry and at huge expense to the government. I was not invited to take part in the bomb's development as I was viewed as being a security risk.

In 1940, I became an American citizen. As I continued my work, I listened with horror to what was happening in the war. In Europe, millions were dying in the gas chambers and concentration camps. What could be done from so far away? One way was to find ways of defeating the country of my birth. Another was to raise money for Jewish charities. This I could do. In 1944, I rewrote my 1905 theory and raised six million dollars.

By 1945, the world's first atomic bomb had been made and although it had been created to use against Nazi Germany, the war in Europe ended and the atomic bomb was not needed. However, the war in Asia against the Japanese was still in progress. On 6th August 1945, an atomic bomb was dropped on the city of Hiroshima and on 9th August a second one was released over Nagasaki, resulting in the end of the Second World War. When we saw the horrific injuries of the people that had been in the two cities, I knew we had to do something to prevent any future use of atomic weapons. In 1946, Szilard and I started the Emergency Committee of Atomic Scientists and we invited six other scientists to join us. The Committee raised money which was spent on informing ordinary people about the effects of radiation from the atomic bombs. We hoped that we could prevent any more bombs from ever being tested or used. By 1951, I was exhausted by the amount of work I had and decided to end the Committee. But this did not mean that its message was no longer being given to people. One of the members was Linus Pauling, who tirelessly continued to campaign for the end of nuclear testing and for nuclear disarmament for many years.

◆ ◆ ◆

Once the war was over, we all breathed a sigh of relief but further problems were to hit me. My son, Eduard, became ill and died in hospital. Mileva had been paying for his care with the result that not only did she have no money, she had also run up large debts. I decided to help but in a mix–up, 85,000 Swiss francs of my money went into her account. Legally, she had the right to keep the money, which of course she did. I didn't try to get the money back. When my other son and his family also moved to the USA, Mileva came with them, but we did not start our life together again and in 1953 she became ill and died.

My own energies were becoming weak and two years later I, too, died. My life had not been easy. One thing was sure, though: I had come up with the theory of relativity that changed <u>perceptions</u> and would set the <u>agenda</u> for a new age.

Einstein in old age

The Life of Albert Einstein

1879   Albert Einstein was born on 14th March in Ulm, Germany.

1880   Albert's family moved to Munich, where his father and uncle set up a company that made electrical equipment.

1884–1894   He was educated at a Roman Catholic elementary school and then continued his education at the Luitpold Gymnasium. Albert's family moved to Pavia in Italy. He joined them later upon completion of his school year.

1895–1896   Aged 17, Albert graduated from Aargau Cantonal School in Aarau, Switzerland. He enrolled at the ETH (the Federal Polytechnic) in Zurich. He also gave up his German citizenship to avoid military service.

1897–1900   He began a four year mathematics and physics teaching diploma at ETH Zurich. He became friends with a classmate, Mileva Maric.

1901   Albert received his Swiss citizenship. He published the paper, *Conclusions from the Capillarity Phenomena*.

1902   He found a job in Bern at the Federal Office for Intellectual Property.

1903   He married Mileva and their son, Hans
        Albert, was born a year later. They had a
        second son, Eduard, six years after that.

1905   Albert published five papers. His paper on
        the Special Theory of Relativity and his
        equation of e=mc^2 made him well known
        in the scientific community. He was also
        awarded a Doctorate from the University of
        Zurich. His dissertation was entitled, *A New
        Determination of Molecular Dimensions*. He also
        published papers on the photoelectric effect,
        Brownian motion, special relativity and the
        equivalence of mass and energy.

1908–1909 He was employed as a lecturer at the
        University of Bern. The following year, he
        accepted the position of physics consultant at
        the University of Zurich.

1911   Albert became a full professor at Karl-
        Ferdinand University in Prague. He also
        worked on his theory of relativity.

1914   He became director of the Kaiser Wilhelm
        Institute of Physics and held that position
        until 1932. He became a professor at the
        Humboldt University of Berlin, Germany.
        His wife, Mileva, remained in Zurich with
        their two sons. Albert became a member of
        the Prussian Academy of Sciences.

1916–1918   *General Theory of Relativity* was published. Albert was made president of the German Physical Society.

1919   On 29th May, a solar eclipse proved his theory of general relativity and he became famous. After he and his first wife divorced, he married Elsa Loewenthal.

1921   Albert began a series of lecture tours in America, England, Asia and Palestine. He was awarded the Nobel Prize in Physics for his explanation of the photoelectric effect.

1925   He was awarded the Copley Medal by the Royal Society. He also joined the Board of Governors at the Hebrew University.

1926   Leo Szilard and Albert co-invented the Einstein refrigerator (patented 11th November, 1930).

1927   He began developing the field of quantum mechanics with Niels Bohr.

1933   Albert emigrated to the United States.

1939   He warned President Roosevelt that Germany might build an atomic bomb. Albert recommended nuclear research.

1940   Albert became a citizen of the USA while keeping his Swiss citizenship.

1944   Albert wrote a copy of his 1905 article on
       the theory of relativity and it raised about six
       million dollars for charity.

1945   The Second World War ended with
       the nuclear bombing of Hiroshima and
       Nagasaki.

1946   Albert became chairman of the Emergency
       Committee for Atomic Scientists, which
       he had started with his friend Leo Szilard.
       In the following years, he worked for
       <u>disarmament</u>.

1950   He published *On the Generalized Theory of
       Gravitation*, where he described his unified
       field theory.

1955   He co-signed the Russell-Einstein Manifesto
       warning of the nuclear threat. Albert died
       aged 76, in Princeton, New Jersey, USA. In
       his lifetime, he published over 300 scientific
       papers and 150 non–scientific papers.

Alexander Fleming

◆ ◆ ◆

1881–1955

the man who discovered the first antibiotic

Chance may have the most amazing influence on our lives. I have one piece of advice to young laboratory assistants – never ignore something that appears to be extraordinary. You never know what it may lead to.

♦ ◆ ♦

I was born on 6th August, 1881. I grew up on a farm in Scotland and apart from the noise that eight children could make, it was a quiet life. My mother, who was 26 years younger than my father, was his second wife and together they had four children. I also had four half-brothers and sisters from my father's first marriage. I was the second youngest of all eight children. My father died when I was only seven years old and when I was fifteen, I moved to London and stayed with one of my brothers, Tom, who was a doctor. I went to the Royal Polytechnic Institution and then I worked in

a shipping office, which I didn't particularly like. However, when I was 20, I <u>inherited</u> some money from my Uncle John, which meant I now had some choices in life. My brother suggested that I went to medical school and this seemed like a reasonable idea. So in 1901, I enrolled as a student at St Mary's Hospital, London.

I worked extremely hard for five years and was lucky enough to graduate with a distinction. I was now a qualified <u>surgeon</u> but I was also interested in the study of bacteria – the tiny living things that cause disease and infections – and St Mary's had a large laboratory. If I had wanted to continue with surgery, I would have had to go to another hospital. A friend introduced me to Sir Almroth Wright, who was a <u>well-respected</u> immunologist, and head of the laboratory. Immunology is the study of how the body becomes ill and how it reacts to disease, and I was fascinated by it. I later heard a rumour that the friend who had introduced me to Sir Almroth Wright did so not because he wanted me to work in the lab, but because he wanted me to stay with the St Mary's shooting club! Had I left St Mary's, I would have been on another shooting team. I never found out if this was the truth or not, but it didn't matter as I wanted to follow this career path anyway, and so I became Sir Almroth Wright's assistant.

Research was a slow but <u>rewarding</u> job and I was content. Sir Almroth Wright was working on producing vaccines to prevent people from becoming ill with diseases. However, in 1914, the Germans invaded France and the First World War began. Doctors were desperately needed so I volunteered and joined the Royal Army Medical Corps as a captain. I was sent off to France to work at the heart of the fighting. Under Sir Almroth Wright, we set up a mobile laboratory in a field hospital – these were temporary hospitals near the fighting – in northern France. The battlefields of the First World War were terrible places and as a doctor, I did what I could, but unfortunately it was usually too little, too late.

The field hospitals were not the clean, quiet hospitals I'd known so far in my medical career. Often they were not much better than the trenches the soldiers were living in and fighting from. Trenches were long narrow holes that the soldiers dug in the ground. They were cold and damp and full of disease. From here the soldiers fought their enemies and here most of them died. Some were killed immediately by a bullet or an explosion, and I soon learned to think of them as the lucky ones. Many more died horrible deaths as their wounds became infected from the deadly bacteria that were everywhere. Even many of those who had surgery, and managed to survive it, died from infections and blood poisoning afterwards. The doctors were trying to stop some of the infections by using antiseptics – these were drugs that killed bacteria – but they were problematic. The antiseptics could not tell the difference between healthy parts of the body with 'good' bacteria and those that were infected.

In our laboratory we were able to study how wounds were becoming infected and we came to the conclusion that the antiseptics were causing more deaths than they were preventing. Our advice to surgeons was to just keep the wounds clean and dry without using any antiseptics. Despite Sir Almroth Wright supporting our <u>findings</u>, field doctors continued using antiseptics and soldiers continued to die unnecessarily. After having seen for myself what damage 'bad' bacteria did to the body, I was determined to go back to my laboratory when the war was over and find some solutions.

In the middle of all this death and destruction, there was also some joy. I became friendly with a nurse working with me in the field hospital. Her name was Sarah Marion McElroy and she was from Ireland. We soon became close and because we knew how valuable life was and that we could be killed at any time, we decided to get married. We were both 34 years old. When the war ended and we had come out of it without injury or disease, we were able to set up home in London. I returned to St Mary's Hospital, as assistant director of the research laboratory this time, and began my search for an antiseptic that would only kill harmful bacteria and not an otherwise healthy person. In the beginning, I focused on the eyes, as tears contain an antibacterial <u>agent</u>, an <u>enzyme</u> called lysozyme, but it was not strong enough to fight other infections, and I continued my search.

♦ ◆ ♦

The birth of my son, Robert, in 1924, pushed me to work harder and harder as one thought kept coming into my head. What would happen if he got ill with an infection that I couldn't cure? We carried out one experiment after another until one day when we made an amazing discovery by chance. I had been on holiday and had left some dishes containing the staphylococcus bacteria I was working on in a corner. The dishes should have been cleaned before I left, but I had been in a hurry and didn't see any harm in leaving them until I came back.

I came into the lab refreshed and ready to start work again and I went over to deal with the abandoned dishes. I noticed that fungus had grown on some of the dishes, which in itself was not anything special. The amazing thing was that wherever the fungus had grown, there was a ring around it that was clear of staphylococcus. It would seem that the fungus had killed the bacteria. I couldn't believe my eyes and we tested over and over again to make sure there hadn't been a mistake. Sure enough, the bacteria were killed every single time by the fungus. We had discovered the world's first antibiotic by accident.

I called the fungus penicillin because under the microscope it looked like a little brush, which in Latin is *penicillus*. It was incredible, as even when it was diluted 1,000 times, it worked. It wasn't only effective with staphylococcus, it attacked the bacteria of many diseases: scarlet fever, pneumonia, meningitis, diphtheria and more. Ironically, it didn't attack typhus – the disease I'd been trying

The formula for penicillin

to find a cure for at the time. In 1929, I wrote an academic paper on the findings and it was published in the *British Journal of Experimental Pathology*. Other scientists and doctors thought my observations were interesting but my work was not taken seriously. My penicillin was sent to chemists for development and we started doing <u>clinical</u> tests, but the results were not encouraging. There were difficulties in <u>isolating</u> the part of the fungus that was killing the bacteria. Then it was proving difficult for the chemists to grow large quantities of it. In the tests, penicillin was being used on surface wounds, like an antiseptic, and this proved to be unsuccessful as it wouldn't stay in the body long enough to be effective. Other projects had priority and for eight years penicillin was abandoned.

♦ ◆ ♦

Then, two doctors from Oxford University, Howard Florey and Ernst Chain, read my paper and did further research, trying penicillin on infected mice. This time the drug would be <u>injected</u>, not applied to the surface of the skin. As I expected, the mice were cured as the bacteria causing their infections were killed. The next step was to try it out on a human subject – would it work if it were injected into a person? In 1942, a policeman became seriously ill after he had been gardening and had scratched himself while cutting his roses. His scratches became infected and the infection spread to his eyes, face and lungs. All the existing conventional treatments had been tried without success, so when he was told about penicillin, he was willing to try it. There wasn't much available but within just a few days, he started to improve. Unfortunately, there wasn't enough penicillin to complete the treatment, the infection came back and the policeman died. However, it was clear that penicillin could work.

♦ ◆ ♦

By now we were in the middle of another world war and medical and military people were beginning to realize the importance of penicillin. There was little money available for research in Britain but luckily Florey had connections in the USA. The biggest problem, as before, was being able to make enough penicillin. Florey and his research team discovered a research centre in Illinois, which was able to grow the penicillin fungus on a type of corn called maize, which was not farmed very much in Britain. The conditions for the fungus to grow were perfect and they were able to produce five hundred times more than had been produced before. In 1943, over 450 million tons of it was produced. Penicillin was not poisonous to anything except certain types of bacteria, and it was cheap to make. Suddenly there was a life-saver for soldiers and citizens alike. It was fast-acting and quickly became a drug that was used widely by doctors to fight their patients' infections.

In 1945, Dr Florey, Dr Chain and I were awarded the Nobel Prize. It was undecided who should get the most credit – myself for accidentally falling on such a great discovery or Florey and Chain for turning my find into the huge success it became. The year before this, I became Sir Alexander Fleming when I was knighted by King George VI. In 1948, I became Emeritus Professor of Bacteriology at the University of London. After my wife died in 1949, I continued working and four years later I found happiness again with Amalia Koutsouri-Vourekas, a Greek doctor, and we got married. Two years later, aged 73, I died at my home in London, knowing that penicillin had saved and was continuing to save millions of lives all over the world.

The Life of Alexander Fleming

1881   Alexander Fleming, known as Alec, was born on 6th August in Ayrshire, Scotland.

c.1887   Alexander attended Loudoun Moor School and Darvel School. He earned a two-year scholarship to Kilmarnock Academy, before attending the Royal Polytechnic Institution in London.

1888   When Alexander was seven, his father died.

1897–1901   He worked in a shipping office for four years. In 1900, he became a member of the Territorial Army in the London Scottish Regiment. He served until 1914.

1901   Alexander inherited a sum of money from his uncle and he decided to study medicine.

1903   He enrolled at St Mary's Hospital Medical School, in Paddington, London.

1906   Alexander qualified with the degree of MBBS (Bachelor of Medicine, Bachelor of Surgery), with distinction, from St Mary's.

1908–1914   He gained a BSc (Bachelor of Science) degree with a Gold medal, after working as the assistant bacteriologist to Sir Almroth Wright, a leader in immunology. Alexander worked as a lecturer at St Mary's Hospital. He was made a Fellow of the Royal College of Surgeons in 1909.

1915   Alexander served as a captain in the Royal Army Medical Corps throughout the First World War. He worked as a bacteriologist and studied antibacterial substances in a laboratory near to the battlefields. He met and married Irish nurse, Sarah Marion McElroy. They later had one son, Robert Fleming.

1918   After the war, he returned to St Mary's Hospital as Assistant Director of the Inoculation Department.

1921   Alexander researched an enzyme which he named lysozyme. This is found in many body fluids including tears.

1928   Alexander was elected as Professor of Bacteriology of the University of London. He made a chance, but significant discovery from a glass dish. The result was the antibiotic substance, penicillin, from the fungus *penicillium notatum*.

1941   During the Second World War, penicillin was mass-produced, which helped treat the wounded soldiers.

1943   He was elected as a Fellow of the Royal Society.

1944   Alexander was knighted by King George VI, as a Knight Bachelor. His colleague Howard Florey was also knighted. He was made a Fellow of the Royal College of Physicians.

1945   He received the Nobel Prize in Physiology or Medicine with Howard Florey and Ernst Chain.

1948   He became Emeritus Professor of Bacteriology at the University of London.

1949   His wife, Sarah, died.

1953   He got married a second time, to a Greek colleague, Dr Amalia Koutsouri-Vourekas.

1955   Alexander died aged 73, in his London home.

Linus Pauling

◆ ◆ ◆

1901–1994

the only person to have won two unshared
Nobel Prizes

**I was actively involved in the development of the atomic
bomb. When I saw the consequences of it being dropped
on Hiroshima and Nagasaki, I spent the rest of my life
trying to stop it from being tested and ever used again.**

♦ ◆ ♦

I was born on 28th February in Portland, Oregon, in the USA.
My father died when I was quite young and my mother had
a difficult time looking after us as we were really quite poor.
I went to the state schools – which were free – in my area. In
1914, while I was at Washington High School, I saw a friend's
chemistry experiment and I immediately became fascinated
with the whole subject. I was lucky to win a <u>scholarship</u> to
Oregon State University – without it, it would have been
impossible for me to go to university at all. Even with the
scholarship, I still had to get a job and I worked all the way

through my years at college, until I got my BSc (Bachelor of Science) degree in chemistry.

While I was at college, I combined studying with teaching. One course I taught was chemistry for students whose main course was home economics. This was a class attended by a lot of girls and no boys. One of the girls, Ava Helen Miller, caught my eye and we became friends. It wasn't long before I decided she was the girl for me and on 17th June 1923, we got married. Life was good, but because we went on to have four children, we were also rather poor.

Meanwhile, after graduating from university, I went to Caltech – the California Institute of Technology. I was interested in the structure of <u>atoms</u> and how they stuck together to form <u>molecules</u>. I started using X-rays to examine the <u>molecular</u> structure of <u>crystals</u>. This work led me to look at the link between physics and chemistry, and I began to apply what was known about <u>quantum physics</u> to chemistry. Using my new theories, I was now able to explain the molecular structure of many things that had been puzzling scientists for years. The discoveries I made in this field allowed many chemicals – <u>dyes</u>, plastics and <u>synthetic fibres</u> that are still being used today – to be developed.

I published seven papers on this subject, got my PhD (Doctorate in Philosophy) in 1925 and was invited to go to Europe to work with some of the great scientific minds of the time. I was given a Guggenheim Fellowship, which gave me enough money to live and study for the whole time I was away. This was an incredible experience for me, but by 1927, I had returned to Caltech as a staff member and became busy with research and experiments. I published 50 papers and established what was known as Pauling's Five Rules. By the age of 30, I became a full professor – a professor at the highest level – as well as continuing with my chemical research. The technical work was going very well but many other scientists questioned whether our <u>findings</u> at Caltech were of any use in real life. What they didn't know at the time were the truly enormous <u>implications</u> of our work, because chemical bonds – the way that atoms are held together – were the basis for a new generation of bomb, the atomic bomb. In 1932, I published what was called the Pauling Electronegativity Scale. The following year, I was elected to the National Academy of Sciences – a great honour as I was the youngest member there. In 1934, I was elected to the American Philosophical Society and in 1935, I published *Introduction to Quantum Mechanics*. Two years after that I became chairman of the Division of Chemistry and Chemical Engineering and director of the Gates and Crellin Laboratories, at Caltech.

◆ ◆ ◆

By 1939, I had written a textbook called *The Nature of the Chemical Bond*. I concentrated fully on my work, finding it fascinating and at home, my wife and I were busy raising our family. Then from the distance came the news of war as the Germans started invading countries across Europe. Up to this point, I had not been involved in politics, but I realized that with my knowledge of chemistry and physics I had to do something, so I started research on <u>explosives</u>.

I was also involved in medical research. A disease called sickle cell anaemia – which makes people ill because it changes the shape of the blood cells – was discovered to be a molecular disease. This of course was within my area of interest and with two colleagues, I was able to produce artificial <u>antibodies</u> to fight the disease. We also had a tremendous breakthrough when we discovered how to make a substitute for blood plasma – the part of the blood that cells live in. As it turned out, I also needed medical attention myself. I had been feeling tired and unwell for some time, more than just serious overwork could explain. Then I was <u>diagnosed</u> with a <u>kidney</u> disease that was often fatal. I was lucky enough to have a doctor who was trying out a new type of treatment that many thought was rather extreme. It involved drinking large amounts of water, and eating little <u>protein</u>. I followed this diet without fail for the next fifteen years and, of course, I didn't die.

In the meantime, the USA had entered the Second World War, when in 1941, the Japanese attacked American soil at Pearl Harbor. On the battlefields, the Germans had been beaten but the Japanese continued to fight and the decision was made to drop atomic bombs on Hiroshima and Nagasaki. From this it became obvious to everyone what could happen when the theory of science, in this case the development of the atomic bomb, was used in real life. <u>Horrified</u> by the injuries caused by this type of bomb, I decided I would focus on how we could prevent war. In 1946, I joined the Emergency Committee of Atomic Scientists, chaired by Albert Einstein. The committee had eight members in total. As a scientist, I knew only too well

An atomic bomb 'mushroom' cloud

what damage exposure to radiation could do, but I saw that the general public were not being told about it.

The ECAS was established to raise money so that the non-scientific community could be informed about the dangers of atomic bombs through lectures and written material. We decided that there were some very basic facts about atomic bombs that scientists worldwide would agree on and that should be made known to everybody. These basic facts were: atomic bombs can be developed so that they can cause more damage in the future. Other countries will also have the technology to be able to invent atomic bombs for themselves and they are not expensive and can be made in large numbers. There is nothing that can be used as a defence against atomic bombs – not now, nor will there ever be in the future. It is not possible for society to prepare for an atomic war. If atomic bombs are used in war, then civilization will be destroyed. The final and most important point was that the only solution is to control atomic energy and how it is used. Even though the ECAS stopped working as a formal organization in 1951, I continued giving speeches about the need for world peace, nuclear <u>disarmament</u> and, for me the most immediate concern, the end of nuclear testing.

However, in 1954, it looked as if more wars were coming, with the Cold War with Russia under way, and the conflict in Korea starting. My views were seen as being <u>unpatriotic</u> by the general population and as a threat by the government, so my passport was taken away from me. At that time I had been awarded the Nobel Prize for Chemistry

A Nobel Prize medal

but now, without a passport, I couldn't go and collect it. Finally, due to pressure from abroad, the government gave in, gave me my passport and I went to Sweden with my family for the award ceremony. I took the opportunity while I was there to get other Nobel winners to support my anti-war cause but when I came back to the USA, trouble was waiting for me.

I had to appear before a government committee to answer questions about my political views. Was I a communist, or had I ever had links with communists? My answer was always 'no' and I continued trying to stop nuclear bomb tests from taking place. On TV and radio and in newspapers, I gave many interviews and almost overnight I became a political figure, even though I had not won an election. Pressure was put on me to reveal the names of other influential people who felt the same way as I did. But, although I was threatened with imprisonment, I refused. After this, my wife and I sent a petition to the United Nations with the signatures of more than eleven thousand scientists demanding the end of nuclear testing. The government couldn't imprison eleven thousand people, many of whom were foreign nationals. In 1962, these activities led to my being awarded another Nobel Prize – this one for Peace. A year later I finally managed to meet President Kennedy, the president of the USA, and tell him my views face-to-face. At the time I wasn't sure if he agreed with me, although he did listen to what I had to say. I must have had some impact because the first nuclear test ban was then announced. This was progress indeed, but I knew I had to keep up the good work.

◆ ◆ ◆

After 42 years at Caltech, I decided to resign and take up a new role to promote democracy and peace. However, I was not happy unless I was doing research, and by now my attention was moving towards health science. In 1967, I became Professor of Chemistry at the University of California, in San Diego and then two years later, I had the same role at Stanford University. In 1970, I published a book that created great interest, *Vitamin C and the Common Cold*. I argued that taking large amounts of vitamin C could reduce the symptoms of a common cold and could even prevent people from catching a cold in the first place. This advice is now taken by millions of people all over the world.

In 1979, with Ewan Cameron, I published another book called *Cancer and Vitamin C* where we suggested that vitamin C had a role in preventing cancer. This theory was not widely accepted but after a great deal of debate, discussion and publicity with TV and radio interviews, it did lead the way to new research into how good nutrition can fight disease. As a result, the Orthomolecular Medicine Institute, where I became director at the age of 72, was renamed the Linus Pauling Institute of Science and Medicine. Ironically, my wife was suffering from cancer and in 1981, she died. Together we had developed a great partnership in the home and against war, and to keep my mind active, I continued working.

I published more books: *No More War!, a 25th Anniversary Edition* and also *How to Live Longer and Feel Better*, which was a title I was trying to live up to as I was, by that time, 85. These were books that everyone could read, not just scientists. New research on vitamin C and AIDS resulted in new treatments being developed, and doctors began looking at the role of vitamins in the treatment of heart disease. Despite having prostate cancer, which I fought with two lots of surgery and huge doses of vitamin C, I lived until the age of 93. Looking back over my life, some people said that I was the Father of Molecular Biology, but I think I would like to be remembered for my efforts to secure world peace.

The Life of Linus Pauling

1901   Linus Carl Pauling was born in Portland, Oregon, USA, on 28th February.

1905   The Pauling family moved to Condon, Oregon.

1910   Linus' father died, aged 33. His mother was left to bring up their three children. She moved and managed a Portland boarding house – a kind of small hotel.

1914   He attended Washington High School. During that time, he saw a friend's chemistry experiment and his fascination for the subject grew.

1917   Linus started studying at Oregon Agricultural College (Oregon State University).

1922   As a senior – a final year student – at university Linus taught Chemistry for Home Economics Majors at the college. A student he taught was Ava Helen Miller. He graduated with a chemical engineering degree and attended the California Institute of Technology (Caltech) in Pasadena, California.

1923   Linus married Ava. They later had three
        sons and a daughter. He published his first
        scientific paper on the crystal structure of
        molybdenite, a soft metallic mineral.

1925   He received his PhD in physical chemistry
        and mathematical physics. During that
        time, he published seven papers. He
        remained at Caltech for the next 38 years.

1926   Linus was awarded a Guggenheim
        Fellowship to study in Munich with
        German physicist, Arnold Sommerfeld,
        Danish physicist, Niels Bohr, in
        Copenhagen and Austrian physicist, Erwin
        Schroedinger, in Zurich.

1927   He returned to Caltech as assistant professor
        in theoretical chemistry and continued his
        research. His 'five rules' were established and
        published two years later as *Pauling's Rules*.

1930   Linus was promoted to full professor at
        Caltech.

1931   The American Chemical Society awarded
        Linus the Langmuir Prize. He published *The
        Nature of the Chemical Bond. III. The Transition
        from One Extreme Bond Type to Another.* The
        following year, he introduced the importance
        of electronegativity and established the
        Pauling Electronegativity Scale.

1933   Linus was elected to the National Academy of Sciences. He was the youngest member to ever be elected. The following year, he was elected to the American Philosophical Society.

1935   He published *Introduction to Quantum Mechanics.*

1937   Linus was appointed chairman of the Division of Chemistry and Chemical Engineering and director of the Gates and Crellin Laboratories, at Caltech.

1939   The Second World War began. Linus published *The Nature of the Chemical Bond.*

1941   Linus was diagnosed with glomerulonephritis, a kidney disease. Because of a new type of treatment given to him by Dr Thomas Addis, he recovered. The American Chemical Society awarded him the Nichols Medal.

1942   Medical history was made when Linus, Dan H Campbell and David Pressman created artificial antibodies. *The Manufacture of Antibodies in Vitro* was published in the *Journal of Experimental Medicine.*

1947   The first edition of *General Chemistry* was published.

1946   Linus joined the Emergency Committee
        of Atomic Scientists, chaired by Albert
        Einstein.

1948   He was awarded the Presidential Medal
        for Merit of the United States. He became
        a foreign member of the Royal Society of
        London.

1949   *Sickle Cell Anemia, a Molecular Disease*
        was published. Linus was president of the
        Scientific Advisory Board of the World
        Union for Protection of Life. He was also
        elected president of the American Chemical
        Society.

1954   Linus was awarded the Nobel Prize for
        Chemistry.

1955   He signed the Russell-Einstein Manifesto.
        The following year, he began to research
        mental illness.

1958   Linus and Ava presented the United
        Nations with a petition. It was signed by
        more than 11,000 scientists, calling for
        an end to nuclear weapons testing. He
        published *No More War!*

1961   He was named Humanist of the Year and
        met with President John F. Kennedy.

1963   Linus was awarded his second Nobel
        Prize, the Nobel Peace Prize for 1962. He
        finally received his high school diploma
        from Washington High School. Linus left
        Caltech and became a staff member at
        the Center for the Study of Democratic
        Institutions in Santa Barbara, California.

1965   *Close-Packed-Spheron Model of the atomic
        nucleus* was published.

1967   He became Professor of Chemistry at the
        University of California, in San Diego.
        Two years later, he served in the same role
        at Stanford University.

1968   Linus was awarded the Lenin Peace Prize.

1970   He published *Vitamin C and the Common
        Cold*.

1973   Linus co-founded the Orthomolecular
        Medicine Institute and was a director. The
        Institute was renamed the Linus Pauling
        Institute of Science and Medicine, in his
        honour.

1974   He co-founded the International League of
        Humanists.

1977   Linus was awarded the Lomonosov Gold
        Medal by the USSR Academy of Sciences.

1979   He was the first person to receive the National Academy of Sciences Award in Chemical Sciences. He was also awarded the Academy of Achievers Award, the Living Legacy Award, and the Gandhi Peace Award. Together with Ewan Cameron, he published *Cancer and Vitamin C*.

1981   His wife, Ava, died of cancer.

1986   *How to Live Longer and Feel Better* was published.

1994   Linus died aged 93, in Big Sur, California, USA.

◆ Glossary ◆

agenda COUNTABLE NOUN
You can refer to the issues which are important at a particular time as an **agenda**.

agent COUNTABLE NOUN
An **agent** is a chemical that has a particular effect or is used for a particular purpose.

antibody COUNTABLE NOUN
Antibodies are substances that your body produces in order to fight diseases.

apprenticeship VARIABLE NOUN
Someone who has an **apprenticeship** works for a fixed period of time for someone who teaches them a particular skill.

arithmetic UNCOUNTABLE NOUN
Arithmetic is the part of mathematics that deals with adding, subtracting, multiplying, and dividing numbers.

atmospheric ADJECTIVE
Atmospheric is used to describe something that relates to the Earth's atmosphere.

atom COUNTABLE NOUN
An **atom** is the smallest possible amount of a chemical element.

benzene UNCOUNTABLE NOUN
Benzene is a clear, colourless liquid that is used to make plastics.

blacksmith COUNTABLE NOUN
A **blacksmith** is someone whose job is making things out of metal, for example horseshoes.

bookbinding UNCOUNTABLE NOUN
Bookbinding is the work of fastening books together and putting covers on them.

botanist COUNTABLE NOUN
A **botanist** is a scientist who studies plants.

chemist COUNTABLE NOUN
A **chemist** is a scientist who studies chemistry.

chlorine UNCOUNTABLE NOUN
Chlorine is a gas that is used to disinfect water and to make cleaning products.

clinical ADJECTIVE
Clinical means involving or relating to the medical treatment or testing of patients.

common cold COUNTABLE NOUN
The **common cold** is a mild illness in which your nose is blocked or runny and you have a sore throat or a cough.

communist COUNTABLE NOUN
A **communist** is someone who supports a political system in which the state controls the means of production, and everyone is equal.

compound COUNTABLE NOUN
In chemistry, a **compound** is a substance consisting of two or more elements.

coordinate TRANSITIVE VERB
If you **coordinate** an activity or information, you organize it.

copper UNCOUNTABLE NOUN
Copper is a soft reddish-brown metal.

crystal COUNTABLE NOUN
A **crystal** is a piece of a mineral that has formed naturally into a regular symmetrical shape.

damp UNCOUNTABLE NOUN
Damp is slight moisture in the air or on the walls of a house.

despair UNCOUNTABLE NOUN
If you feel **despair**, you feel that everything is wrong and that nothing will improve.

diagnose TRANSITIVE VERB
If someone or something **is diagnosed as** having a particular illness or problem, their illness or problem is identified.

dilute TRANSITIVE VERB
If a liquid **is diluted**, it is mixed with water or another liquid in order to make it weaker.

disarmament UNCOUNTABLE NOUN
Disarmament is the act of reducing the number of weapons that a country has.

doctorate COUNTABLE NOUN
A **doctorate** is the highest degree awarded by a university.

dye VARIABLE NOUN
Dye is a substance that is used to change the colour of something.

eclipse COUNTABLE NOUN
When there is an **eclipse** of the sun, the moon is between the Earth and the sun, so that part or all of the sun is hidden.

electrical tension VARIABLE NOUN
The **electrical tension** of an electrical current is its force measured in volts.

electro-magnetic induction
UNCOUNTABLE NOUN
Electro-magnetic induction is the process by which electricity or magnetism is passed between two objects or circuits without them touching each other.

element COUNTABLE NOUN
An **element** is a substance such as gold, oxygen, or carbon that consists of only one type of atom.

empire COUNTABLE NOUN
An **empire** is a group of countries controlled by one powerful country.

enzyme COUNTABLE NOUN
An **enzyme** is a chemical substance that is found in living creatures which produces changes in other substances without being changed itself.

explosive VARIABLE NOUN
An **explosive** is a substance or device that can cause an explosion.

exposure UNCOUNTABLE NOUN
Exposure to something dangerous means being in a situation where it might affect you.

findings PLURAL NOUN
Someone's **findings** are the information they get as the result of an investigation.

foundation COUNTABLE NOUN
The **foundation of** something such as a belief or way of life is the idea or experience on which it is based.

fungus (fungi) VARIABLE NOUN
A **fungus** is a plant that has no flowers, leaves, or green colouring, such as a mushroom or mould.

gas chamber COUNTABLE NOUN
A **gas chamber** is a room that has been specially built so that it can be filled with poisonous gas in order to kill people.

generator COUNTABLE NOUN
A **generator** is a machine that produces electricity.

geologist COUNTABLE NOUN
A **geologist** is someone who studies the earth's structure, surface, and origins.

gravity UNCOUNTABLE NOUN
Gravity is the force which makes things fall when you drop them.

Great Depression PROPER NOUN
The **Great Depression** was a period in the 1920s and 1930s when there was very little economic activity and a lot of unemployment and poverty.

honorary ADJECTIVE
An **honorary** title or membership is given as a mark of respect to someone who does not qualify for it in the normal way.

horrified ADJECTIVE
If someone is **horrified**, they feel shocked or disgusted.

implication COUNTABLE NOUN
The **implications of** something are the things that are likely to happen as a result of it.

influential ADJECTIVE
Someone who is **influential** has a lot of influence over people or events.

inherit TRANSITIVE VERB
If you **inherit** something such as a situation or attitude, you take it over from people who came before you.

inject TRANSITIVE VERB
To **inject** someone **with** a substance such as a medicine means to use a needle and a syringe to put it into their body.

innovator COUNTABLE NOUN
An **innovator** is someone who introduces changes and new ideas.

interpretation VARIABLE NOUN
An **interpretation** of something is an opinion of what it means.

introverted ADJECTIVE
Introverted people are quiet and shy and find it difficult to talk to other people.

ironically ADVERB
You use **ironically** to draw attention to a situation that is odd or amusing because it involves a contrast.

iron ore UNCOUNTABLE NOUN
Iron ore is rock from which iron can be obtained.

isolate TRANSITIVE VERB
To **isolate** something means to separate it from things of the same kind.

kidney COUNTABLE NOUN
Your **kidneys** are the two organs in your body that filter waste matter from your blood and send it out of your body in your urine.

Légion d'honneur
COUNTABLE NOUN
The **Légion d'honneur** is the
highest honour that can be given
in France.

lighthouse COUNTABLE NOUN
A **lighthouse** is a tower near or in
the sea that contains a powerful
flashing lamp to guide ships or to
warn them of danger.

light wave COUNTABLE NOUN
A **light wave** is the way in which
light signals travel.

magnet COUNTABLE NOUN
A **magnet** is a piece of iron that
attracts iron or steel towards it.

magnetic ADJECTIVE
If something is **magnetic**, it has
the power of a magnet or
functions like a magnet.

mass VARIABLE NOUN
The **mass** of an object is the
amount of physical matter that
it has.

melt TRANSITIVE VERB,
INTRANSITIVE VERB
When a solid substance **melts**, or
when it **is melted**, it changes to a
liquid because of being heated.

microscope COUNTABLE NOUN
A **microscope** is an instrument
that magnifies very small objects
so that you can study them.

mineral COUNTABLE NOUN
A **mineral** is a substance such as
tin, salt, or coal that is formed
naturally in rocks and in the
earth.

molecular ADJECTIVE
Molecular means relating to
molecules.

molecule COUNTABLE NOUN
A **molecule** is the smallest
amount of a chemical substance
that can exist.

multiply TRANSITIVE VERB
If you **multiply** one number **by**
another, you calculate the total
that you get when you add the
number to itself as many times
as is indicated by the second
number.

natural philosophy
UNCOUNTABLE NOUN
Natural philosophy was the
study of nature and the physical
world, before modern science
was developed.

Nazism UNCOUNTABLE NOUN
Nazism was the political ideas
and activities of the German
Nazi Party.

nutrition UNCOUNTABLE NOUN
Nutrition is the process of
taking and absorbing nutrients
from food.

occupy TRANSITIVE VERB
If a foreign army **occupies** a country, they move into it, using force in order to gain control of it.

perception COUNTABLE NOUN
Your **perception** of something is the way that you think about it or the impression you have of it.

physicist COUNTABLE NOUN
A **physicist** is a scientist who studies physics.

power TRANSITIVE VERB
The device or fuel that **powers** a machine provides the energy that makes the machine work.

pray INTRANSITIVE VERB
When people **pray**, they speak to God in order to give thanks or to ask for help.

principle COUNTABLE NOUN
The **principles** of a particular theory or philosophy are its basic rules or laws.

protein VARIABLE NOUN
Protein is a substance that the body needs and which is found in meat, eggs, and milk.

quantum physics UNCOUNTABLE NOUN
Quantum physics is the study of the behaviour of atomic particles.

radiation UNCOUNTABLE NOUN
Radiation is very small particles of a radioactive substance. Large amounts of radiation can cause illness and death.

radioactive ADJECTIVE
Something that is **radioactive** contains a substance that produces energy in the form of powerful rays which are harmful in large doses.

ray COUNTABLE NOUN
Rays are narrow beams of light or heat.

recognition UNCOUNTABLE NOUN
When a person receives **recognition** for the things that they have done, people acknowledge the value or skill of their work.

refreshed ADJECTIVE
If you feel **refreshed** after feeling tired, hot, or thirsty, you feel more energetic or cooler.

rewarding ADJECTIVE
Something that is **rewarding** gives you satisfaction or brings you benefits.

scholarship COUNTABLE NOUN
If you get a **scholarship** to a school or university, your studies are paid for by the school or university, or by some other organization.

sewage UNCOUNTABLE NOUN
Sewage is waste matter such as faeces or dirty water from homes and factories, which flows away through underground pipes.

spark COUNTABLE NOUN
A **spark** is a flash of light caused by electricity.

static electricity UNCOUNTABLE NOUN
Static electricity is electricity that is caused by friction and that collects in things such as your body or metal objects.

surgeon COUNTABLE NOUN
A **surgeon** is a doctor who cuts open people's bodies to repair or remove diseased or damaged parts.

synthetic fibre COUNTABLE NOUN
Synthetic fibres are thin threads made from chemicals or artificial substances rather than natural ones.

unpatriotic ADJECTIVE
Someone who is **unpatriotic** does not love their country and does not feel very loyal towards it.

well-respected ADJECTIVE
If someone is **well-respected**, a lot of people have a good opinion of their character or ideas.

zinc UNCOUNTABLE NOUN
Zinc is a bluish-white metal that is used to make other metals such as brass or to cover other metals such as iron to stop them rusting.

Collins
English Readers

Agatha Christie

THE MAN IN THE
BROWN SUIT

THE MYSTERIOUS
AFFAIR AT STYLES

APPOINTMENT
WITH DEATH

THE MURDER OF
ROGER ACKROYD

The Queen of Crime for
English Language Learners

Twenty Agatha Christie Mysteries

CEF Level B2 • incl. CD

historical and cultural notes • character notes
glossary • online support

www.collinselt.com/agathachristie

Collins
English Readers

ALSO AVAILABLE IN THE AMAZING PEOPLE READERS SERIES:

Level 1

Amazing Leaders
978-0-00-754492-9
William the Conqueror, Saladin,
Genghis Khan, Catherine the Great,
Abraham Lincoln, Queen Victoria

Amazing Inventors
978-0-00-754494-3
Johannes Gutenberg, Louis Braille,
Alexander Graham Bell, Thomas Edison,
Guglielmo Marconi, John Logie Baird

Amazing Entrepreneurs and Business People *(May 2014)*
978-0-00-754501-8
Mayer Rothschild, Cornelius Vanderbilt,
Will Kellogg, Elizabeth Arden, Walt
Disney, Soichiro Honda

Amazing Women *(May 2014)*
978-0-00-754493-6
Harriet Tubman, Emmeline Pankhurst,
Maria Montessori, Hellen Keller, Nancy
Wake, Eva Peron

Amazing Performers *(June 2014)*
978-0-00-754508-7
Glenn Miller, Perez Prado, Ella
Fitzgerald, Luciano Pavarotti,
John Lennon

Level 2

Amazing Aviators
978-0-00-754495-0
Joseph-Michel Montgolfier, Louis
Blériot, Charles Lindbergh, Amelia
Earhart, Amy Johnson

Amazing Architects and Artists
978-0-00-754496-7
Leonardo da Vinci, Christopher Wren,
Antoni Gaudí, Pablo Picasso, Frida Kahlo

Amazing Composers *(May 2014)*
978-0-00-754502-5
JS Bach, Wolfgang Mozart, Giuseppe
Verdi, Johann Strauss, Pyotr
Tchaikovsky, Irving Berlin

Amazing Mathematicians *(May 2014)*
978-0-00-754503-2
Galileo Galilei, René Descartes, Isaac
Newton, Carl Gauss, Charles Babbage,
Ada Lovelace

Amazing Medical People *(June 2014)*
978-0-00-754509-4
Edward Jenner, Florence Nightingale,
Elizabeth Garrett, Carl Jung, Jonas Salk,
Christiaan Barnard

Level 3

Amazing Explorers
978-0-00-754497-4
Marco Polo, Ibn Battuta, Christopher Columbus, James Cook, David Livingstone, Yuri Gagarin

Amazing Writers
978-0-00-754498-1
Geoffrey Chaucer, William Shakespeare, Charles Dickens, Victor Hugo, Leo Tolstoy, Rudyard Kipling

Amazing Philanthropists
(May 2014)
978-0-00-754504-9
Alfred Nobel, Andrew Carnegie, John Rockefeller, Thomas Barnardo, Henry Wellcome, Madam CJ Walker

Amazing Performers *(May 2014)*
978-0-00-754505-6
Pablo Casals, Louis Armstrong, Édith Piaf, Frank Sinatra, Maria Callas, Elvis Presley

Amazing Scientists *(June 2014)*
978-0-00-754510-0
Antoine Lavoisier, Humphry Davy, Gregor Mendel, Louis Pasteur, Charles Darwin, Francis Crick

Level 4

Amazing Thinkers and Humanitarians
978-0-00-754499-8
Confucius, Socrates, Aristotle, William Wilberforce, Karl Marx, Mahatma Gandhi

Amazing Writers *(May 2014)*
978-0-00-754506-3
Voltaire, Charlotte Brontë, Mark Twain, Jacques Prevert, Ayn Rand, Aleksandr Solzhenitsyn

Amazing Leaders *(May 2014)*
978-0-00-754507-0
Julius Caesar, Queen Elizabeth I, George Washington, King Louis XVI, Winston Churchill, Che Guevara

Amazing Entrepreneurs and Business People *(June 2014)*
978-0-00-754511-7
Henry Heinz, William Lever, Michael Marks, Henry Ford, Coco Chanel, Ray Kroc

Collins
English Readers

Also available at this level

Level 4
CEF B2

Amazing Thinkers and Humanitarians
978-0-00-754499-8

Amazing Writers
978-0-00-754506-3

Amazing Leaders
978-0-00-754507-0

Amazing Entrepreneurs and Business People
978-0-00-754511-7

Sign up for our emails at **www.collinselt.com**
to receive free teaching and/or learning resources, as well as the most
up-to-date news about new publications, events, and competitions.

⒠ POWERED BY COBUILD

www.collinselt.com

 @CollinsELT

 /collinselt